WHAT ARE THEY
SAYING ABOUT
YOU?

BIS Publishers
Building Het Sieraad
Postjesweg 1
1057 DT Amsterdam
The Netherlands
T +31 (0)20 515 02 30
F +31 (0)20 515 02 39
bis@bispublishers.com
www.bispublishers.com

ISBN 978 90 6369 400 5

Text and concept: Frank Peters
Design and concept: Sara van de Ven

WHAT ARE THEY SAYING ABOUT YOU?

50 lessons to manage
your personal reputation

Frank Peters

B/S

TABLE OF CONTENTS

BUILD YOUR REPUTATION

PROTECT YOUR REPUTATION

INTRODUCTION

"You are what is said about you after you have left the room"....
that is your personal reputation. And that reputation is beco-
ming increasingly important. Not only professionally, but definitely also personally. Whether you are the manager of an
organisation, a specialist in a hospital or the director of your
own company.

A good reputation distinguishes you from the rest and therefore
creates opportunities. At the same time, your reputation is also
more fragile than ever. We have increasingly started to pay
attention to others and are called out on our actions. Or indeed
our lack thereof. But that is not all, as our stakeholders judge
us more severely and personally for our behaviour. In short: we
are observed with a more critical eye than before, judged and,
if necessary, publicly sacrificed. In this social media era, every
day is 'judgement day'.

It is not only our stakeholders that have become more critical,
for instance due to all the scandals in the past ten years. The
current social media era has made the world increasingly more
transparent and increasingly less remains hidden. Moreover,
pressure is easily organised. That can be arranged with one
targeted tweet.

With these developments the pressure on all of us has thus increased. Before you know it, you suffer from personal damage: legal, financial or to your reputation. However, this time also offers opportunities if you are aware of the possibilities and the laws of reputation management.

This book offers 50 lessons for building and protecting your personal reputation. These lessons are based on my experience of 30 years of reputation management and crisis consulting for brands, organisations and people.

This book is meant for anyone who realises that reputation is important and would like to take matters into their own hands. Don't hesitate to consider this book your personal spin doctor. If you take these lessons to heart, you create distinction and will be protected by your reputation cushion for now and later, if it comes to that.

Frank Peters

1. EVERYONE IS A BRAND

Everyone is a brand. Not just companies such as McDonald's and Apple. Or well-known people such as Mark Zuckerberg and Madonna. You, too, are a brand. Nowadays, if you wish to know something about a person, company or brand you only need to enter their name into Google. The results then pop up instantly: publications, articles, blogs, but also photos and profiles on LinkedIn, Twitter and Facebook. A great portion of that content comes from others. Go ahead and Google yourself for once. You will then know what is being said about you on the Internet.

Your stakeholders gather an impression of you, whether you like it or not. And in doing so, they determine your brand. Or indeed your reputation. You will have to manage that process in order to get it moving into your desired direction. And everything starts with the awareness that you yourself need to take over the steering wheel. Management guru Tom Peters already recognised this back in the nineties of the previous century. He said: "Regardless of age, regardless of position, regardless of the business we happen to be in, all of us need to understand the importance of branding. We are CEOs of our own companies. Our most important job is to be head marketer for the brand called You."

2. KNOW WHAT YOU STAND FOR

Naturally, if you wish to manage your own brand, you will have to think of how you wish to be regarded by your environment. You need to ask yourself what your identity is. Or: Who am I? What am I capable of? What do I wish to mean to others? What distinguishes me from others? And especially: Why do I do the things I do? Subsequently, it is important to consider what personal (brand) values correspond to this; what is it that characterises you and what do you believe in?

Thus, your identity indicates who you are, what drives you and what your days are dedicated to. It is the story you tell people about yourself and the basis for what you publish online about yourself, for instance. And, greatly important: what makes you different from the rest!

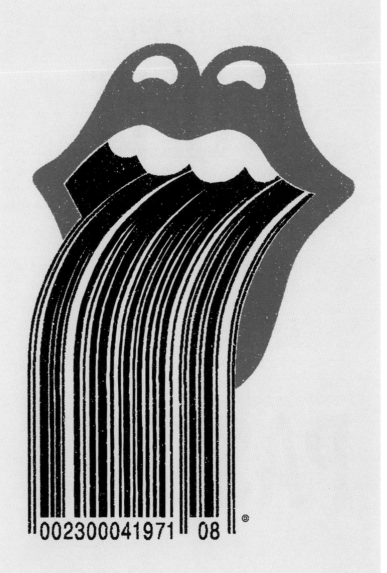

DO IT WITH PASSION

OR NOT AT ALL.

Passion is a crucial factor for your own identity. Television star Oprah Winfrey recognises the power of passion: "Passion is energy. Feel the power that comes from focusing on what excites you." Let your passion lead you in the choices you make. And remain true to your focus, because consistency is the prerequisite for communicating your identity and establishing your brand.

3. CREATE YOUR OWN STORY

If you know what you stand for, then it is effective to translate this into a captivating story. 'Storytelling' may seem fashionable, but it has been around during all ages. The Bible was passed on by the telling of stories.

Virtually all successful managers are masters in the use of stories. Storytelling connects work to the soul. It is precisely with stories that you can bring your passion and personal drives to life. Stories make everything more personal, and thus more human. When a good story is told, you remember the message much more easily and the story will be passed on much more quickly. You could actually consider many of the historic speeches to constitute a form of storytelling. Martin Luther King with his speech "I have a dream" from 1963 is still one of the most beautiful examples of this.

Elements that need to be reflected in your story are: What is your drive? What do you stand for? What are you aiming for? What challenges do you or have you faced? What were your personal milestones? How would you like to be perceived by your stakeholders? Make it simple, relevant and at the same time as objective as possible.

Of course, your story must also be told. You can do so online and offline. You can use text, but increasingly often stories are told with images: photos or videos. Nothing works as effectively as video, because it allows you to really convey emotions. Consider the success of YouTube.

You can tell your own story. But you can also have staff members, partners or customers do this for you. In all cases, ensure that the story is authentic and do not practice self-aggrandizement. Ultimately, it is about creating a passionate story that is worthy of sharing and is capable of deepening and strengthening relationships.

4. REMAIN AUTHENTIC

Authenticity is essential for communicating your identity. If you pretend to be different than you are, your stakeholders will soon see through you. Apple's CEO Tim Cook declared in 2014 that he is gay and was praised for his openness by friend and foe. You do not have to come out of the closet tomorrow in order to receive the same response. Start with concentrating on who you truly are and what you are good at naturally. And be clear and honest about that. That forms the basis for the image that people on the outside will construct of you. Of course, it does need to be close to reality. Henry Ford, founder of the Ford Motor Company, rightly concluded: "You can't build a reputation on what you are going to do." Naturally, there can be ambition in your identity. But it is important to remain yourself and not pretend that you are someone different from who you really are. That is unnatural and dangerous. After all, you will have to be able to confirm your story with your behaviour daily.

At the same time, you can show that you are also just human. Showing your vulnerable side and making mistakes indicates that you are authentic and not perfect. After all, nobody is perfect! Be aware of that, provide information and show yourself.

5. BELIEVE IN YOURSELF

The more you believe in yourself, the bigger the chance that positive things will happen in your life and others start believing in you. Learn from the challenges that you face and think positively from the perspective of opportunities. In doing so, operate from your own strength and what makes you unique in comparison to others. Always apply positive thinking. Or, as the always self-confident boxing legend Muhammed Ali already indicated: "It's lack of faith that makes people afraid of meeting challenges. I believed in myself." So, stand for who and what you are. In that manner, you will also strengthen the image that you would like to communicate to your stakeholders.

6. THE ART OF LETTING GO

Your reputation is what the outside world thinks of you and, unfortunately, that is usually not in accordance with how you view yourself. It requires constant work to bring those two worlds closer together. Take into account that the image the outside world has of you always equals reality. Your stakeholders determines your reputation, not you! Only your own behaviour can be an instrument in getting your reputation as close as possible to your desired image. Former Chief Evangelist of Apple, Guy Kawasaki, provided the tip in his book *Enchantment*: "Be a Mensch". His advice was simple: Ensure that you are open, transparent and friendly. That is the basis for any relationship. Not only private, but certainly also professional.

Realise that is it impossible to have full control over what happens in your environment and what people think of you. Resign to the increasing unmanageability in this digital age. You yourself are no longer in the driver's seat.

7. CLAIM YOUR NAME ONLINE

Nowadays, your reputation is usually made or broken online. Therefore, make sure you are visible and active online. Claim your own name on e.g. Facebook, Twitter, LinkedIn and Google+. It offers you the chance to use these channels yourself and ensure that you are found if anyone looks for you. However, you also prevent misuse, as others could communicate in your name from these platforms.

Richard Branson, founder of Virgin, is a classic example of the social CEO. Since 2007, he has already been active on Twitter and has millions of followers. However, he is still an exception in the world of CEOs. Most managers do not get much further than creating a LinkedIn profile. And that while social media can help you create a more personal, empathic and transparent profile. Those are important factors for gaining trust. Follow Richard Branson's example. And, of course, you can also do so with fewer followers.

8. YOUR STAKEHOLDERS HOLD THE POWER

Nowadays, stakeholders hold the power over the image that is formed of people and brands. This presents a threat, but also opportunities.

For instance, in 2008, email and social media such as Twitter and YouTube were used on a great scale for Obama's election campaign in the United States. In order to best inform his supporters, Obama and his campaign team made use of these channels. Not the media, but the subscribers of his newsletter and Twitter followers received the latest developments first and then shared those. It ensured a strong sense of connection with Obama and ultimately more donations for the campaign. Politics 2.0 was born. Thus, the social media environment took over an important part of the work for team Obama. And we all know what the result was: victory for the democrats and the election of the first black president in the history of the US.

The fact that your stakeholders can also make things quite difficult for you, is clearly demonstrated by the case of fashion brand Abercrombie & Fitch (A&F). In 2013, statements from Mike Jeffries, the CEO of A&F, were made public concerning the fact that his brand is not meant for fat women and that he therefore offers no sizes bigger than Large in the shop. The world did not accept this. Emotional responses and rage were the result. The brand was hacked and customers turned their back. With all the associated consequences. Jeffries eventually left at the end of 2014, after much criticism and poor financial results.

Realise that absolute control over your reputation is an illusion. Resign to the fact that the power lies with others. Therefore, invest time and attention in relationships with the outside world. And do not forget your enemies in this. It is best to keep them close-by.

9. LISTEN TO LEARN

The most important prerequisite for managing your reputation is listening to what people think of you. It is not about listening to react, but listening to learn. So you must hear what the other is saying, but also try to understand what the other means. Only then will you know what you can do with this information. And this will lead to an understanding of what you need to do to change your image and gain the trust of others. Moreover, it offers you insight into the role you can play in the outside world. Of course, this is not easy, as it is easier to do the talking and try to convince someone else of your point of view. Try a different approach. It will yield valuable results, because every relationship begins with listening to the other. Indeed, it is the very foundation!

Listen to your environment by asking people how they view you and what they think of you. And make sure that you listen to what is said about you on blogs, social media and forums on the Internet. Monitor your own name. You can easily do that with free services such as Hootsuite, Mention, Social Mention and Google Alerts. You can enter various keywords and will automatically receive updates when those show up.

LISTEN

&

SILENT

are spelled with

the same letters

Think about it :)

10. ARM YOURSELF FOR BATTLE

If you wish to prevent problems, you need to know where you are vulnerable. Look into the mirror and make an inventory of where risks are lurking. Think of the worst that can happen to you. Not only for your organisation, but also for yourself. Then estimate the chance that those risks will present themselves to you and what impact this could have on your reputation. You will have to protect yourself against the risks that carry the biggest impact and probability. Think about the tactics and communication for the most realistic and sensitive risks. In short: prepare a pre-emptive defence before another person gets a chance to open fire. Ensure that you are ready to communicate quickly and adequately. For instance, with a core message that can serve as a basis for a press release and email to internal and external stakeholders. In addition, an FAQ document and inventory of the most important stakeholders for various risks. As an organisation, you will practice a crisis situation with a sensitive risk at least once a year. Review periodically whether the preparation is still up-to-date and whether other risks have presented themselves.

Thus, never be taken off guard. The success lies in the preparation, not in the execution.

11. INFLUENCE YOUR IMAGE ON GOOGLE

Anyone who wants to know something about you will check Google. Whatever the first page on Google shows, will be considered the truth. Therefore, it is important to regularly check how you score on Google. You then know what your status is with the outside world. And that is the image you need to actively influence. You can help create your desired image on Google by posting neutral and positive content yourself, linking to influential news sites, blogging for important websites, or receiving recommendations from others. That is how you secure increased online visibility.

However, that can also work against you, of course. Seeing as everything on Internet remains documented. For instance, Google still shows many images of the biting incident involving the footballer Louis Suarez. These pictures overshadow his qualities as a top athlete. It takes great efforts to neutralise a negative image.

12. BUILD 'FRIENDSHIPS' IN TIMES OF PEACE

It is not until bad times arrive that you learn who your real friends are. Everyone who has ever gone through a crisis before knows this. And practice indicates that you will usually find yourself alone.

If you want to be able to rely on friends in a crisis, you will need to build relationships in times of peace. Think of who are important stakeholders for you. In thinking about this, also consider the possible risks that you face and which stakeholders are involved in these. Invest in an open dialogue with them. Tell them what you are working on and what challenges you face in the process. Friendship will not always be the result, but you can definitely count on a greater sense of understanding and less resistance. Moreover, it is interesting to look at common interests and opportunities for creating alliances. When it comes to it, you will have a more solid position. Frank Underwood poignantly phrased this in the television series House of Cards: "Winners build bridges. Losers build Walls."

13. BUSINESS AND PRIVATE ARE ONE!

It is important to realise that you can no longer separate professional from private in this age in which everything can be found online. Increasingly more often, employees are fired or job applicants are rejected due to what they post on social media. Be aware of what traces you leave on the Internet and know that they are virtually inerasable. Thus, think twice before you publish that ill-considered post on Twitter or that compromising photo on Facebook. They do your reputation no good.

TRUST IS LIKE A PAPER

ONCE IT'S CRUMPLED

IT CAN'T BE

PERFECT AGAIN

14. TRUST IS THE NEW CURRENCY

Trust has become a rare commodity. Worldwide consumer confidence is at a historic low. Particularly crises and scandals, such as problems with the banks, are the cause of this. Not only the business world, but also the government is distrusted nowadays. At this time, people mainly trust the opinion of their friends, family and well-known opinion leaders in the market.

If you succeed at gaining the trust of your stakeholders, you create a foundation for relationships. In practice, trust comes down to the sum total of transparency, integrity and honesty. It is therefore best to make those principles leading in your behaviour and communication.

15. DUMP YOUR EGO

Your ego makes for a very poor counsellor in reputation management. Society no longer accepts ego-tripping. If the outside world does not like it, they vote with their feet. And they will announce this to the entire world with a big fat #*fail.*

Thus, say goodbye to personal interest and make yourself secondary to the goal you wish to accomplish. Opt for the role of connector in this network society and invest in relationships with your stakeholders. And, in doing so, certainly do not avoid your 'enemies'. Invite the others into dialogue and interaction. It may seem like a slowing of your pace, but you will be able double your speed as a result.

The discrepancy between global footballers Messi and Ronaldo is a good example of the effects of an oversized ego. Barcelona star Lionel Messi distinguishes himself in terms of quality and modesty. Therefore, he is respected by friend and foe. Not only due to his success, but also because of the person he is and how he behaves. Despite all his success, opponent Cristiano Ronaldo of Real Madrid can only look on with envy. Thanks to his inflated ego, he remains in the shadow of his rival.

FREE

AIR BAG

TESTING

POINT

16. CULTIVATE A REPUTATION CUSHION AS AN AIRBAG

If you know who you wish to be, then you will also have to communicate that. Make a calendar with communication activities and put them into action. Build relationships with those who are important stakeholders for you. Not only friends, but indeed also enemies. Then work on your visibility, for instance by means of a good website and active use of social media such as Twitter, LinkedIn and Facebook. But also build your authority by speaking at conferences and giving workshops. Or writing blogs and articles in relevant media. This way, you create distinction and cultivate your reputation cushion, which serves as an airbag for less favourable times.

17. LIVE YOUR BRAND

It is a mistake to think that you are ready once you have a nicely worked out story. In fact, it is a huge misconception. For that is only the first step in the process. Your story and personal (brand) values will only carry meaning if they are brought to life. Building your reputation requires a permanent investment. Especially in good times, you will constantly have to stay occupied with it. You will have to become the personification of your brand. By continually telling and carrying out your (brand) story and personally living it with a great deal of passion. Day in, day out!

Former top manager Steve Jobs from Apple was a striking example of living the brand. He was Apple and Apple was Steve Jobs! He was extremely consistent in carrying out his identity and that of Apple's. In stark contrast are the examples of actor Charlie Sheen from the television series Two and a Half Men in 2011 and presenter Jeremy Clarkson from the car programme Top Gear in 2015. Both were eventually fired due to personal misconduct, with which they not only damaged their own reputations, but also those of their successful programmes.

18. EMOTION IS NOT FOR LOSERS

Showing emotions is often seen as a weakness. That is a huge misunderstanding. Because rationality hardly counts in reputation management anymore. Empathy and display of emotion is increasingly considered a strength. CEOs such as Howard Schultz from Starbucks and Jeff Bezos from Amazon.com are famed for their keen eye for emotion. They prioritise their relationships with their own people and customers in word and deed. For instance, Schultz speaks openly about his love for the company and his people.

Your intelligence quotient (IQ) is no longer leading. Emotional intelligence (EQ) has become just as important. Naturally, you cannot fake emotion. You need to always be natural and authentic. But make sure you have a keen eye for emotion in your stakeholders and treat it with understanding. And if necessary, choose to show vulnerability. That takes away tension and results in a base of support.

19. SEEK OUT THE DIALOGUE

The times of exclusively broadcasting in communication have definitively come to an end. Communication was actually always about a two-way stream, but we still like to convince others of our opinion. That time has gone. Your stakeholders do not just want to be informed, but wish to be actively involved. They have an opinion and wish to express their view on how you operate as a person or organisation. Therefore, you need to be prepared for that. Because if you ignore this desire, you will end up facing some difficulties. For your communication, use channels that enable the dialogue. Social media such as Facebook and Twitter are excellent vehicles for this. The same goes for blogs. Do not fear the responses and adversity. Instead, enter the discussion with an open attitude. That will result in understanding and respect from the outside world. Moreover, the dialogue will give you insight into what is going on in the world around you, which will allow you to take that into account.

20. HONESTY LASTS THE LONGEST

Ultimately, lies are always exposed, but the truth will always remain true. Honesty, like openness, is an important prerequisite for building your personal reputation. Indeed, it is crucial for obtaining and maintaining trust. Therefore, do not paint a prettier picture than reality and do not conceal anything either. Eventually it will surface. Thus, do not lie about your occupation or your CV. Scott Thompson, CEO of Yahoo, was caught doing that a number of years ago. He claimed also to have obtained a university degree in computer sciences. In reality, he only studied accounting. The lie was exposed, Thompson was suspended and his reputation was severely damaged.

When you face problems or crises it is equally important to always communicate honestly. Under pressure from your stakeholders, fact-finding is always the central focus and they will eventually get to the bottom of the matter. It is better to count on that from the start.

21. TRANSPARENCY IS THE NEW BLACK

Transparency is the magic word. WikiLeaks is one of the advocates of transparency in our society. Founder Julian Assange is of the opinion that the more power one has, the greater the need is for transparency. For if power is abused, it has huge consequences. Naturally, the ultimate goal must always be maximum openness. However, at the same time, saying too much can have a paralysing effect. After all, the other parties need to be able to understand and handle the information.

Your stakeholders ultimately determine whether or not you are transparent enough. And that has everything to do with the confidence they have in you. The less trust they have, the more openness is required. It is clear that the call for transparency makes demands on your communication. Always consider carefully how open you need to be. In your communication, strive to achieve the greatest degree of transparency, for eventually the truth always rises to the surface. When that happens, you are better off being the messenger of the information.

22. HOLD ONTO YOUR VALUES

Consistency in behaviour is a prerequisite for realising your desired reputation. Not only in your words, but especially in your actions, hold onto the values of your personal brand. Not only does that apply in good times, but certainly also in bad times. It is very tempting to let go of one of your values every now and then, if that suits you a bit better in the short term. However, ultimately you will be held accountable for those deviations and every day will turn into 'judgement day'. The current transparency age and the social media tools give your stakeholders the insight and power to see, judge and exercise pressure. Deviating from your values will come at the expense of your credibility and your reliability.

The values are like a lighthouse for your behaviour and help you in making decisions. Therefore, you need to visibly live them. It will help you to be seen as the person you would like to be and achieve your goals and dreams. However, it also strengthens your leadership. And once the storm does hit, your values offer a beacon for ultimately staying the course.

23. UNDER-PROMISE, OVER-DELIVER

Management guru Tom Peters considers it the formula for every success: "under-promise and over-deliver!". In the currently crowded market it is difficult to stand out. This often leads us to promising much more than we can actually deliver in practice. Which causes the problem that you end up not meeting the expectations you created yourself. Peters holds the opinion that this is definitely the wrong route to take. His advice is to distinguish yourself precisely in terms of reliability. Sticking to agreements has never been as important as in this time of uncertainty. You truly make a difference if you then proceed to even deliver that bit more than the other party is expecting. This is actually about realism, honesty and proper expectation management. Just refrain from promising too much and always honour your agreements. That creates confidence and strengthens your reputation.

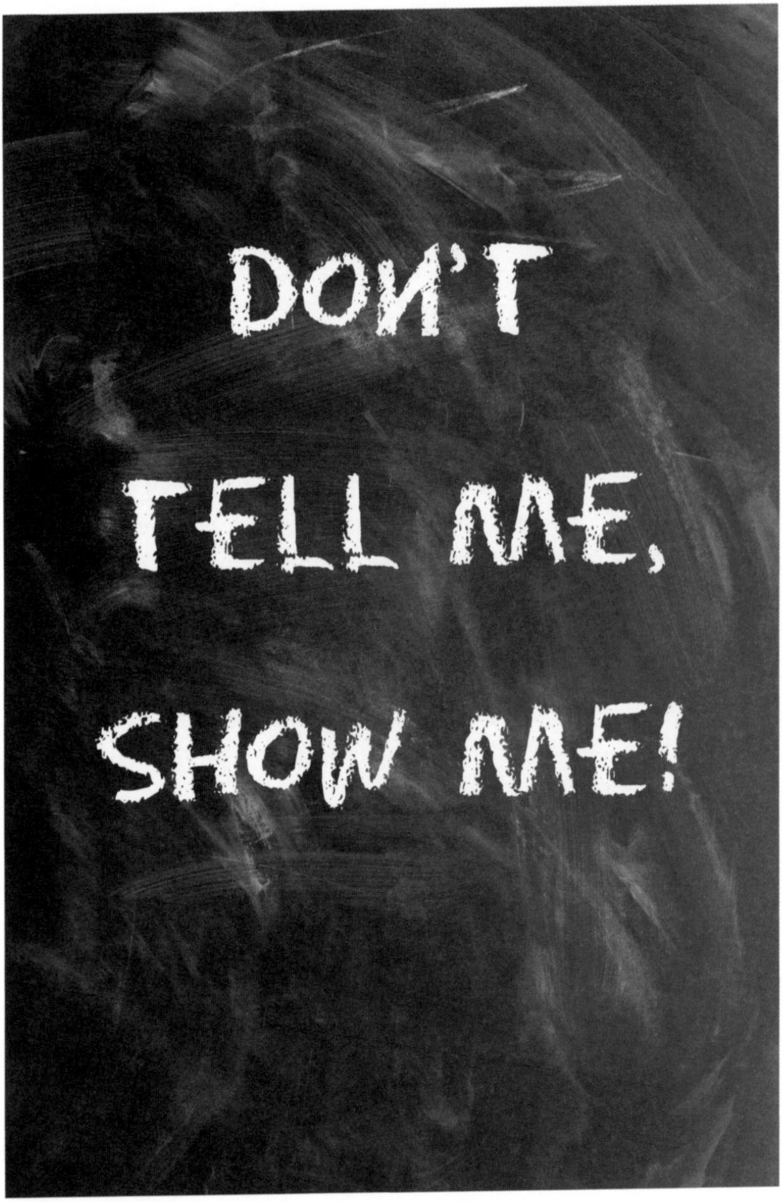
DON'T
TELL ME,
SHOW ME!

24. SHARE SUCCESSES WITHOUT EXAGGERATING

Naturally, you need to tell your story yourself. You can do this through your personal communication throughout e.g. networks built online and in the real world.

'Be Good and Tell It' reads an old expression from the public relations world. These days, 'Be Good and Prove It' is rather more fitting. In other words, your reputation is determined by what you do and not what you say. On a daily basis, you will have to prove to the outside world that you are making your desired reputation a reality. Thus, provide hard evidence. It is important to share successes with the appropriate amount of pride. However, do not paint a prettier picture than reality. Exaggerating is counterproductive.

25. MAKE SURE OTHERS TALK ABOUT YOU

Better than communicating yourself is having other people tell the story for you. For instance, your own staff members or customers as ambassadors. In communication this is also referred to as positive word of mouth (WOM). That is always more credible than when you yourself are speaking. Nowadays, people buy what their friends and family buy. Make use of that. Back in the day, Walt Disney said about the power of WOM: "Do what you do so well that people can't resist telling others about you."

Word-of-mouth promotion is increasing in importance at a time in which the confidence in entrepreneurs is at a historic low. Even the number of likes on your Facebook page or the number of followers in Twitter work as 'recommendations'.

Ensure that you activate others to communicate about you. For instance, by inviting satisfied customers to write reviews. Or by supplying interesting or humoristic content they can spread online. In addition, it is important to facilitate staff members in telling the right story to the outside. Therefore, you need to provide them with sufficient information and space for posting on social media about work. Moreover, it is important to know who are important 'influencers' in your market. Build a relationship with them and inform them about who you are and what you do, and offer them interesting information they can distribute. Finally, it is important to invest in your own position of authority. In other words, become an 'influencer' yourself. For instance, by writing a blog or twittering about your field of expertise. In short: create content that is worth passing on.

DANGER   OPPORTUNITY

危機
危机

A TIME OF   A TIME OF
DANGER   OPPORTUNITY

26. A CRISIS ALSO OFFERS OPPORTUNITIES

In Chinese the word 'crisis' has two definitions: 'danger' and 'opportunity'. Very often, crises are only viewed from the perspective of a threat. Naturally, it is essential to be aware of the dangers of a crisis. After all, first attention will be dedicated to avoiding or limiting personal reputation damage due to the crisis. The recovery of reputation damage after a crisis takes on average three to four years. And it can even cost you your head. At the same time, it is also interesting to look at the opportunities. This does not only concern the lessons and the room for improvement.

Crisis offers an occasion to demonstrate that you are well capable of handling tricky situations. If you act decisively, open and effectively, a crisis can even have a positive effect on your reputation. Particularly in bad times, you have the chance to show what you are worth and what you stand for. Crisis offers you the chance to demonstrate leadership and take responsibility. And if you do, that commands respect. If you neglect to do so, then your stakeholders will deal with you without any mercy.

27. DO AWAY WITH CRITICISM ON SOCIAL MEDIA

Nobody is perfect and everyone makes mistakes every now and then. Therefore, it is logical that you will receive criticism on social media sooner or later. You do not have to panic when you do. Do not ignore the feedback and refrain from immediately closing your Twitter or Facebook account. Instead, take the criticism or commentary on social media serious. After all, on average Twitter users have a few hundred followers and the same goes for friends on Facebook. If someone shares a negative experience, this will quickly spread like an oil spill, creating a 'mob' that can make your life quite difficult. Before you know it, a complaint can grow into a reputation crisis. It is important that you deal with criticism or a problem openly and show what you are doing to solve it.

There is a simple approach to adequately dealing with questions and criticism on social media: listen, solve, follow up. Of course, it starts with listening. You will have to be quick to identify whether there is a problem. It is all about responsiveness; responding quickly and adequately to possible violations to your reputation. Make sure that you check social media at least once a day. Preferably a number of times per day. You then need to offer solutions to problems that have been reported. And it is important to also follow up afterwards. A few days onwards, check whether the problem has indeed been solved and whether the 'complainer' is satisfied. Should the atmosphere on social media truly be hostile, then choose for a highly personal approach, if necessary inviting the 'complainer' to send you an email or call you. You can then offer a solution one on one. Airline company KLM promises its customers a response to their questions and complaints within 48 minutes. In ten languages and in every time zone. In doing so, they became trendsetters in the field of international web care.

Question
or request?

KLM
Royal Dutch Airlines

We expect to reply within:
48 min.
Updated every 5 minutes

28. DENIAL IS THE BIGGEST RISK

Denying an impactful issue or a crisis is one of the biggest dangers to any reputation. Former General Electric CEO Jack Welch is of the opinion that a feature of good leadership is to quickly deal with the problems of crises. He recommends searching for a solution immediately. Acknowledging the problem is the first step towards a solution. Take care of a quick reaction and especially actions. And do not forget to share these with your stakeholders. Everyone will then know that you are taking your responsibility. Beautiful words alone are not sufficient. Your stakeholders want to see that concrete action is taken and that decisive intervention is taking place. You are better off overreacting quickly, than responding too late or not at all. The manner in which you respond to a crisis influences the general opinion of you for years to come. In positive, but especially negative ways!

29. TAKE YOUR RESPONSIBILITY

"There's no one who wants this thing over more than I do, I'd like my life back" were the words that signalled the downfall of BP executive Tony Hayward. He made this statement to journalists after the occurrence of the oil spill in the Gulf of Mexico. Hayward, who had to come back from his sailing holiday, was accused of egoism and mercilessly judged for these words. Because the rest of the world did not have any understanding and was waiting for his sense involvement and an actual explanation for this disaster.

Take responsibility for the crisis and show that you mean it. You will have to accept the situation in order to do so. Therefore, admit to what has gone wrong, if necessary offer your apologies, and demonstrate what you are doing to solve it and prevent a recurrence. In doing so, also indicate what the planning looks like and when you will offer new information again. If you do not, then your stakeholders will be merciless and your reputation will soon be over and done with. After all, you build your reputation by continually being able to meet the expectations of the internal and external stakeholders.

30. DELIVER BAD NEWS YOURSELF

A good offence is still the best defence. Never allow yourself to be surprised by bad news about yourself. If you have a problem, announce that to the outside world yourself. In doing so, you determine the moment and the manner in which the world is informed. In the field of communication this tactic is referred to as 'Stealing Thunder'. You force your stakeholders to react instead of the other way around. Moreover, it is the only way in which you maintain the control in the communication. Make sure the ball is in your court and you choose the offence: that is the basis for managing a crisis. Or, as soccer legend Johan Cruijff once said: "If we have the ball, they can't score".

Thus, it is important to draw a clear and factual picture of the crisis at the very start. Meet the information needs of your stakeholders yourself. The starting point for your communication should always be the wellbeing and the safety of your stakeholders. And thus not your own reputation or the financial consequences of the crisis. That is of later concern.

31. THERE IS NO SUCH THING AS "NO COMMENT"!

There is no worse response than "No comment". Bad news always continues, with or without your response. Therefore, waiting until all the facts are known is not an option. If you do not explain what is going on yourself ('crisis framing'), then others will do so for you. Everyone with a smartphone has become a journalist and can create news within a matter of minutes. But also the traditional media will go in search of the story themselves. And that increases the chance of incorrect information circulating and the risk of constantly having to do damage control. With all its consequences. At the start of a crisis, it is often not yet possible to answer substantive questions. But that always leaves the option of providing a process-focused response and explaining what you are doing to solve the problem. That is credible and creates confidence. Ducking and postponing is not an option. It is certainly not necessary to have all the answers at the start of the crisis. However, always indicate when you do expect to have those answers.

em·pa·thy

The ability to
identify with or
understand
another's
situation or
feelings:
Empathy is a
distinctly human
capability.

32. SHOW UNDERSTANDING TO RECEIVE UNDERSTANDING

Compassion is important in a crisis. Demonstrate involvement and communicate empathically and avoid being defensive. Pay attention to your tone of voice and body language.

Always speak from the perspective of the people involved instead of your own. Show understanding for emotion, anger or fear in your stakeholders and demonstrate this in your response, too. Ultimately, you will need to develop an eye for the impact of your actions on another. For instance, regarding their safety. If someone has been injured, you need to demonstrate that you 'feel' that pain yourself. The place where you share your response is also crucial. Compassion at a distance carries less value. When the Virgin Galactic crashed in 2014, CEO Richard Branson flew directly to the place of disaster to be with his team. Moreover, he immediately responded on social media with a first sign of solidarity.

33. BEING RIGHT
≠
WINNING THE ARGUMENT

You know you are right, but your stakeholders have a very different opinion. This will cause you to be at direct odds with one another every now and then. If you wish to accomplish something, you thus need to go with the flow. Take one step back in order to be able to take two steps forward. Only then will you eventually win the game. Therefore, stay focused on the result you wish to achieve.

Take into account that emotions are currently prevalent in crisis situations. You will no longer win the game with rational arguments. The time of 'being right is winning the argument' has long gone. You will need to cultivate an eye and understanding for the emotions of others. Communicate with understanding. Thus, more along the lines of 'soft communication'. The purpose of communication is not convincing, but connection. Vulnerability and emotion are a sign of the times.

34. DILEMMAS CAN BE SHARED

In the past, there was a prevailing consensus that you should always radiate power. Thankfully, that line of reasoning has changed. It is not a weakness to share dilemmas with the outside world. In fact: it is increasingly expected. This does mean, however, that you need to dare to show your vulnerability. Vulnerability can bring us closer together. Just like in your day-to-day life, this can also be useful for managing your reputation. Go ahead and involve your stakeholders in the questions you need to solve and provide insight into the difficulty and time it costs you to do so. This creates understanding. Sometimes it is even good to actively involve stakeholders in finding the right or maximum solution. It can yield unexpected insights and help create a base of support for the choices you make.

35. FIGHTING IS DONE TOGETHER

When you are facing problems, you learn who your real friends are. Not only does that apply for your private life, but certainly also professionally. Therefore, it is important to know your friends and enemies, so you know who you will be facing when you encounter problems. Map the stakeholders. And build relationships with them in times of peace, because otherwise they will not be much use to you in times of a crisis. Or, as Michael Corleone already said in *The Godfather II*: "My father taught me: keep your friends close, but your enemies closer." Corleone understood it well. Opponents have more understanding for you if there is an open relationship. And friends can provide extra support and help 'neutralise' the opponents. Ultimately, you will often be by yourself in times of crisis, but support helps lighten the load.

36. ONLY RELY ON YOURSELF

In unfortunate times you learn who your real friends are. And previous experience in crisis situations teaches that you will virtually always be on your own when it truly comes down to it. Be aware of that in determining your tactics for managing a problem situation. Of course, it is important to consider from where you might receive support or with whom you could even enter into an alliance. You definitely need to make use of that. But once it really gets tense, you will eventually be left to your own devices. Therefore, it is advisable to only rely on yourself and not fully count on the support from others for solving an issue or crisis.

37. RUBBING A STAIN?

'If you rub a stain, it only becomes bigger' is a much-used expression in crisis communication. It is important to think twice before you start rubbing your own stain. For if you are not careful, you will only make the trouble bigger.

Therefore, you really need to think before you push back. If you have a good story, immediately come out with it and take control in the communication. But if you do not, then it can sometimes be better to simply "sit still while you are being shaved," as the Dutch proverb says. In those cases, going along with the predominant discourse can be best.

IT TAKES 20 YEARS TO BUILD

A REPUTATION, AND ONLY

5 MINUTES TO RUIN IT.

IF YOU THINK ABOUT IT,

YOU'LL DO THINGS DIFFERENTLY.

— WARREN BUFFETT

38. THE POWER OF ACTIONS

Having gained wisdom through shame and scandal, American top entrepreneur Warren Buffett aptly stated: "It takes twenty years to build a reputation and five minutes to ruin it." You can take as long as you want to build your reputation, but ultimately you will be judged by the speed and the way in which you deal with unexpected situations. Results achieved in the past will then no longer count. Everything is about your action at the moment things get tricky. If you then respond too late or poorly, you can forget about it. An adequate and quick response is in your own interest. In the current social media era the response times at moments of crisis have sometimes been reduced to just a few minutes. Thus, you have no more time to lose.

39. MAKE THEM AN OFFER THEY CANNOT REFUSE

If you have caused problems, then you will also have to solve them. That is the golden rule of crisis management. Because otherwise the crisis will continue. For instance, if you are demonstrably responsible for people having suffered risk or damages, you arrange for compensation. For example in the form of a new product or covering costs. Or by repairing the damage suffered. Take no risks, especially when you cannot guarantee the health or safety of your stakeholders. Act immediately and take measures.

Besides, careful communication with those affected is already half the solution. For instance, patients judge the overall quality of a medical specialist virtually completely on the basis of the communication process. Even in case of a mistake. In practice, not taking victims serious and poor communication often escalates into unnecessary legal actions and claims.

40. TELL ALL AND DO IT QUICKLY

Nowadays, everyone with a smartphone has become a journalist and crises usually spread across the entire world within one hour. Therefore, you are forced to react immediately. Which you should, because you are better off taking care of the framing of the crisis situation yourself. You then maintain control and determine the picture of the crisis yourself. If you do not, another person will do it for you and you will be placed in the position of having to defend yourself. Thus, make sure that you provide information very quickly. And reveal as much as possible in doing so. This demonstrates that you have the situation under control. If you do not have facts yet, then at least share what you are doing in order to solve crises.

AirAsia top executive Tony Fernandes took immediate and compassionate action when, at the end of 2014, one of his airplanes disappeared. He predominately used Twitter for this as a news medium. And he then continued to send updates. In addition, there was immediate proactive and open crisis communication, in which he also explicitly sought out the dialogue with his stakeholders. Actor Bill Cosby chose not to actively communicate in the crisis surrounding the sexual accusations made against him. He let himself be caught off guard and was publicly sacrificed while he kept silent.

IMPORTA

MESSAG

41. KEEP IT SIMPLE

Formulating short and clear messages is important for making communication effective. That always applies, but especially in case of problems and in crisis situations. Therefore, communicate in spoken language and avoid the use of technical jargon. And, in doing so, think from the outside in. Moreover, research shows that the use of strong language increases the effect of your message. Words such as 'beautiful' and 'awful' are much more convincing than 'appealing' or 'unappealing'. It is important that you, as the source, are credible to the receiver. Otherwise, the communication will be counterproductive. Moreover, the message has a greater effect when you communicate from the problem towards the solution.

Therefore, you need to carefully consider the framing of your messages. In short, the framing always consists of three phases:

1. LOOK: this is going on (painting a picture of the problem with understanding for the emotion that has emerged because of it).
2. BECAUSE: this has happened (explanation of the facts and responsibility).
3. SO: this is what I will do to solve it (offer perspective).

42. SPECULATION IS DISASTROUS

In March 2015, Lufthansa was confronted with an airplane accident of their subsidiary Germanwings in the French Pyrenees. All 150 passengers died in that crash. CEO Carsten Spohr indicated after the dramatic incident that his copilot had been 100% fit to fly. However, later it became clear that his employee had been under medical treatment and had presumably crashed the aircraft on purpose. Despite the positive support for Lufthansa's crisis communication, this statement had been clumsy.

The basic rule for external communication in crisis situations is that you should only provide factual information. In short: only facts that are 100% certain. Of course, it can be very tempting to speculate. For instance, about the cause of a crisis situation or the question of blame. Nevertheless, if you are not certain, then remaining silent on the matter is the best option. After all, it is disastrous if you speculate, only to have the actual facts catch up with you later on. You then need to retract your statement and that leaves a dent in your credibility. Thus, do not start guessing and assuming. However, do communicate. But focus on the events, the consequences and how you will deal with those. Only when you have investigated everything and know the facts, then you can proceed with the next substantive communication step.

Apologizing doesn't always
mean that you're wrong and
the other person is right. It just
means that you value your
relationship more than your
ego. - Unknown

43. SAYING SORRY DOES NOT HURT

Sorry seems to be the hardest word was once a big hit by the British singer Sir Elton John. And with good reason, as everyone will recognise the sentiment. In practice, it is a big problem for many. Even though apologising does not always mean that you were in the wrong. Often, it simply indicates that your choose the value of a relationship or friendship above your own ego.

Should you make a real mistake along the line, ensure that your apology contains at least the following elements: Admit that you were wrong, accept liability for it, indicate that you regret what has happened and promise that it will not happen again. Only offering your apology is never enough in itself. It needs to be accompanied by concrete actions. Indicate what you are doing to solve the mistake or crisis and how you intend to prevent it in the future. When the new CEO of General Motors, Mary Barra, had just taken up her position in 2014, she was already faced with managing her first crisis: a recall of 1.7 million cars. Barra and her advisors chose to film a personal apology. In front of millions of viewers she admitted: "Something went very wrong...and terrible things happened." Media praised her transparency and action. Especially because CEOs usually tend to duck in times of crisis.

44. SHOW WHAT YOU ARE DOING

When you are under pressure, it is important to offer a clear picture of the situation. Not only of what is the matter, but also of what you are concretely doing to change it. Be realistic and do not paint a prettier picture than reality. Not even from a place of opportunism or an optimistic attitude. Instead, realise that your stakeholders wish to influence the process. Therefore, it is important to actively involve them. Align the objective and the solution and follow on social media whether your stakeholders are satisfied. You know you are golden when you see the sentiment change from negative to neutral or even positive.

45. BENDING OR BURSTING

The tendency to offer a rational defence in response to an attack often occurs in crisis situations. For instance, take the bankers in the financial crisis. They were pointed at with an accusing finger, because they had known – or were supposed to have known – that irresponsible risks had been taken. However, most of them did not give an inch and subsequently became the target of public opinion. It is a natural response to directly want to disprove your opponent's view. However, this is not always the correct strategy. Experience teaches that merely hard and rational confrontations often do not lead to the desired goal. Especially not when there is much sensitivity and emotion involved in the crisis situation. Instead, you will really have to take this into account. Because otherwise reputation management turns into amputation management. And you will then most probably find yourself the victim.

In a crisis, it is important to not only want to deflect, but also to give in when it comes to issues for which that is necessary and possible. Understanding for the emotions in your stakeholders and acknowledgement of the emerged situation are important for then creating your own room to clarify your position, standpoints and actions. Going with the flow and sometimes even 'bending' does not constitute defeat. In fact, it is often necessary in order to then emerge stronger from the battle. It does take courage. Showing vulnerability is not a shortcoming, but a distinctive leadership quality. Especially in such times, when emotion rules and your stakeholders are increasingly critical and outspoken. Not bending might then mean bursting.

46. BE THE ONE TO CLOSE THE CRISIS CHAPTER

Formally closing off a crisis is often neglected. Which leads to the danger that with every new 'incident' the crisis is revived again. For instance, a car brand that needs to make an adjustment to its cars, like Toyota at the time. If you then neglect to eventually declare "We have now seen and adjusted all cars", the crisis will keep resurging upon each accident with a Toyota. Therefore, you need to clearly signal when a crisis situation has been completed. When it is once again time for 'business as usual'. Naturally, it is important to not do that until all promises have been delivered on and the pressure from your stakeholders and the media has subsided. Thus, you need to determine for each crisis which steps you need to take to recover from it. And then communicate them openly, too. Later down the line you can always refer back to that. In doing so, you also make the end of the crisis clear.

The End.

47. PROMISES ARE SACRED

Crises will often force you to make promises. After all, in case of fault, you will have to promise improvement in the future. And not to mention also start executing concrete actions in order to bring the crisis to an end. Carefully consider this, for promises create a debt. Especially, make sure not to make any promises for which you already know in advance that you will definitely not be able or willing to deliver on them. For it is lethal to be called out on empty promises after the crisis. In that case, the crisis will return and confidence in you and among the stakeholders will not have benefitted from the promises made.

A MISTAKE
REPEATED MORE
THAN ONCE IS
A DECISION

48. LEARN FROM YOUR MISTAKES

Nobody likes to make mistakes. Yet, you also need to dare to make mistakes in order to become a better reputation manager. As long as you learn from them. Therefore, you should evaluate each crisis that you get caught in and ensure that you do better next time. Moreover, make sure that you take measures in order to prevent the mistakes that caused the crisis in the future. For a mistake that repeats itself will be deemed a decision.

Of course, you can also learn from others' crisis situations. For instance, that of the management of the pizza chain Domino's a few years back. It took them two days to take an act from two of their employees – who did disgusting things during the preparation of their orders – on YouTube serious. Ultimately, the employees were sent packing, but the damage had already been done. The action and the apology from the management came too late. The video of the employees already had attracted more than one million viewers and had been edited and shared again and again. That created a lot of negative buzz for the brand on social media. Direct intervention and firm distancing from the events are the only remedy against reputation damage. That is not only a lesson for Domino's to learn, but for anyone else. Follow the news with a critical eye and learn from the blunders and best practices of others.

49. FIGHT YOUR WAY BACK IN

For a long time, Tiger Woods seemed the ideal role model for top sports. He won everything there was to win, had an excellent reputation and, according to Forbes, was the first athlete to exceed the income threshold of 1 billion dollars. Everything changed in 2009, when his wife kicked him out of his house because he had cheated on her. Woods admitted that he was a sex addict and had slept with over 120 women. His reputation was done with and he lost sponsors such as Accenture and AT&T, and with them a great deal of income. Repairing a reputation takes time. On average recovery takes about three to four years after a severe crisis. In addition to time, recovery also requires visible effort. Show your vulnerability and publicly distance yourself from what went wrong. Promise improvement and take demonstrable steps to resolve the situation and prevent repetition. And, finally, ensure that what you have promised also actually happens and periodically ask your stakeholders for feedback. Everyone deserves a second chance, but usually a third chance is not given. Therefore, you need to make sure that you take your chance at reputation recovery serious. Make it the moment for a fresh new start and approach it with a positive attitude. Despite the fact that his athletic performance leaves something to be desired, Tiger Woods has returned to being one of the highest-earning athletes in the world.

50. ARRANGE FOR A MAJOR CLEAN-UP

If there is anyone who knows how long a personal crisis can haunt you, it is Monica Lewinsky. Google her name and seconds later a million results pop up on the sexual relationship she had with her boss Bill Clinton. In 1998, the affair made the front page of every newspaper in the world and the details were also relayed in all dimensions. Social media such as Twitter did not yet exist, but back then the Lewinsky scandal was already big news on the Internet. Despite a crisis being well behind you, it can still give you grief for a long time to come. Especially on Internet and social media, a crisis remains visible for a long time. It is good to realise this. But it is more important to get active after a crisis yourself to clean the Internet again. You first need to ensure that neutral and positive content once again appears on the Internet. You can also encourage others to contribute to this. This offers a counterweight to the negative reports in the Google search results.

And when there is true nonsense about you on Google, you can submit a request with them to remove it. If necessary, through legal means. In Europe, the judge has now issued a first decision in which it acknowledges the 'right to be forgotten' and that search machines can be obligated to remove results that violate your right to privacy. In addition, demonstrably wrong or hurtful information on other websites can be fought. Approach the owners of these websites and ask them to remove the information. Do not simply remove negative reviews or comments on social media. First solve the problem and ask the people involved to remove their own comments. If you are not able to manage by yourself, you can also hire a specialised agency to clean up the Internet for you.

FURTHER READING

Many interesting books have been written on managing reputations and crisis communication. If you are truly interested, I can warmly recommend some of my favourites:

DIGITAL ASSASSINATION by Richard Torrenzano and Mark Davis. A fascinating and up-to-date book that concentrates on protecting the reputation and organisation against undesired online attacks.

ENCHANTMENT by Guy Kawasaki. Interesting book of this online master. His most important and simple advice: "Be a Mensch". As a brand, be Honest, Transparent and Friendly. That is the basis for everything.

MANAGING CRISES BEFORE THEY HAPPEN by Ian Mitroff. An interesting book that mainly offers context for managers of companies.

MANAGERS GUIDE TO CRISIS MANAGEMENT by Jonathan Bernstein. Mainly a practical book for the application of crisis management in the daily practice. With many checklists.

ONGOING CRISIS COMMUNICATIONS by Timothy Coombs. Standard reference work for crisis communication. In addition to planning and managing a crisis, this book gives much attention to crisis response.

REPUTATION MANAGEMENT by John Doorley and Helio Fred Garcia. A broad and practical book on reputation management from all facets. With much attention for best practices.

SPIN SUCKS by Gini Dietrich. Book on the approach of communication and reputation management in our digital age. The book offers tips on the way in which you can communicate authentically, openly and honestly in order to gain the trust of your stakeholders.

STAKEHOLDER POWER by Steven Walker and Jeffrey Marr. An interesting book on the power of stakeholders and the manner in which that power can be used to the advantage of your organisation instead of against you.

THE BRAND YOU by Tom Peters. A classic in the field of personal branding. Peters was the founder of brand thinking for people.

THE REPUTATION ECONOMY by Michael Fertik and David Thompson. A book on managing our digital reputations as the most important asset in our daily life. With tips and tricks to partly keep your 'digital footprint' hidden to those who are looking for you.

TRUST AGENTS by Chris Brogan. A book on online reputation management and the questions of how you can identify so-called 'trust agents' and get them on your side to create confidence for your organisation through them.

WILD WEST 2.0 by Fertik Thompson. Just like 'Digital Assassination' a gripping book on protecting and repairing the online reputation of an organisation.

CREDITS

ABOUT THE AUTHOR

Frank Peters has been working as an advisor in the fields of reputation management and crisis management for about 30 years. He is the owner of the Dutch agency Virtus Communications. He formerly headed the Dutch branch of the international PR network Porter Novelli. Frank has a great deal of experience in managing high-profile corporate brands and developing corporate communication strategy. He counsels communication management teams and boards of directors at prominent companies. He has received multiple international communication awards for his consultancy work.

Frank is the author of the book *Reputation under Pressure* on reputation management and crisis communication and teaches these fields to various business schools and educational institutions.

THANK YOU

Many thanks to Cesar Moerman and my business partner Eric Heres for their critical eye during the creation of this book. And of course Caroline, Julia and Maarten for their support and inspiration during the writing process. Finally, Rudolf van Wezel of BIS Publishers, who understands that reputation management is important for everyone and has therefore made the publication of this book possible.